live
LOVE
Dream

60 days for

CWR

Contents

Hello Beautiful!

So glad you decided to pick up this book. Every page holds more answers (from the Bible) about who you are, how special you are and what on earth you're here for! Every day read the Bible passage and notes, which show just how helpful and important God's Word is for your life today.

So we start with **Mirror Mirror on the Wall**. This section is all about self-image, confidence and beauty (inside and out). Then in **A Girl Called Ruth** we follow a girl in the Bible, not surprisingly called Ruth. Her story is pretty extraordinary – and a bit romantic too! ☺ Next **Testing! Testing!** gets serious. Life isn't always a bed of pretty pink roses so how do we face the tough times as Christians? **Search for a Star** follows another Biblical heroine: Esther. We see how God had complete control over her life and how He looks after us as well. You may know your fruit of the Spirit off by heart, but **Fruit Salad** unpacks what these really mean for us today. Finally **Get Up and Glow** does what is says on the bottle – get ready to turn your light on and show the world Jesus!

Enjoy!

Mirror Mirror on the Wall

'For you created my inmost being; you knit me together in my mother's womb. I praise you because I am fearfully and wonderfully made; your works are wonderful, I know that full well. My frame was not hidden from you when I was made in the secret place, when I was woven together in the depths of the earth. Your eyes saw my unformed body; all the days ordained for me were written in your book before one of them came to be.' **PSALM 139:13–18**

When you look in the mirror are you pleased with everything you see? How do you view yourself? Many people think they're not worth much, but God wants us to know that we're incredibly special. He loves us and He has good plans for our lives.

The comedian Woody Allen said, 'I have only one regret in life: that I was not born someone else!'

It is a sad fact that many people do not like themselves. Many dream, 'If only I was ...'.

Before you find fault with yourself, take a look at how God sees you. You are not another human blob from some mass production line. You are wonderfully made. A genuine original. **Totally unique. The one and only you!**

God has assembled you from a DNA blueprint He designed. You are custom made by God to be you and no one else. And God has packaged us with instructions so we can get the most out of the life He has given us. More than that, He cares about us and thinks about us all the time. When David got a handle on this fact he took time out to thank God for putting him together so well.

Instead of queuing up at God's complaints counter asking for a refund, we should thank Him that **we are a limited edition** – one of one – ONEderful!

Engage

You are a one-off because you are designed to fulfil a specific purpose in history – a purpose that no one else can completely fulfil. That's right, God has stitched His designer label on your life. Talk with Him and thank Him that you are special.

Pray

Thank You, God, for making me unique. Thank You that whatever everyone else thinks, You think I'm special. Amen.

Whose are you?

'Then God said, "Let us make mankind in our image, in our likeness, so that they may rule over the fish in the sea and the birds in the sky, over the livestock and all the wild animals, and over all the creatures that move along the ground." So God created mankind in his own image, in the image of God he created them; male and female he created them ... And it was so. God saw all that he had made, and it was very good.' **GENESIS 1:26–31**

Do you want the ground to open up when people point out how much you are like one of your parents or relatives? 'She's got her father's ears ...' – oh help! And your ears grow by an average of 0.22mm a year! Hold on! You have a likeness to Someone who won't embarrass you.

When a child reminds us of her parents, we call her a 'chip off the old block' – that is, made of the same stuff as her mum or dad; for better or worse. In some ways we are made of the same stuff as our earthly grandparents and parents, but these amazing verses in Genesis tell us that we have some features similar to our Father in heaven – Almighty God. This does not mean we look like God on the outside, but that we share in some of His honour. We have a soul, we have authority over His creation and we know right from wrong.

We are not sophisticated apes. Well, you can probably think of a few who act a bit like ... er, no, only kidding! God created the human race to be distinct from all other life forms. He created people to be able to communicate with Him and enjoy His friendship forever. Tragically, Adam and Eve blew it by being disobedient. But those who believe in Jesus have the privilege of God living in their lives.

Don't ever put yourself down by telling yourself you're no good: that's an insult to God. We have **God's likeness** in us and that **gives us great value and worth.**

Engage

Just as a coin has the image of a king or queen on it, so Christians have the imprint of God on their lives. Jesus is the 'exact likeness' of God, and the more we become like Him the more we will honour God in our lives. Thank God for Jesus and talk through the areas of your life where you need to become more like Him.

What's her secret?

'The LORD said to Samuel, "... I am sending you to Jesse of Bethlehem. I have chosen one of his sons to be king ... Do not consider his appearance or his height ... The LORD does not look at the things people look at. People look at the outward appearance, but the LORD looks at the heart." ... Jesse had seven of his sons pass before Samuel, but Samuel said to him, "The LORD has not chosen these." So he asked Jesse, "Are these all the sons you have?" "There is still the youngest," Jesse answered ... So he sent for him and had him brought in ... Then the LORD said, "Rise and anoint him; this is the one." So Samuel took the horn of oil and anointed ... David.'

1 SAMUEL 16:1–13

Did you know that more than 90% of girls want to change at least one aspect of their physical appearance? Before you start proceedings to sue your parents for damages, take a look at the way God sees you.

Between the ages of 9 and 21 our bodies go through more changes than at any time of our lives. It's a great temptation to keep comparing yourself with everyone else – or worse, with models in magazines or on TV, and other media personalities. Give yourself a break!

We also get caught up with an 'I want to be different so I'll dress the same as all my friends' attitude, even if it winds our parents up. We find ourselves being very sensitive to comments others make about our appearance. We can feel rejected if others don't find us 'attractive'. As we look into the eyes of others to see what impression we are making, our confidence can grow – or take a crushing.

God doesn't see us as being too tall, too short, too fat or too thin. **He accepts us just as we are.** But He does want us to have an inner beauty that shows on our face and through our actions. God is concerned about our looks – He wants us to look up before looking around.

Engage

God wants to give you a 'beautiful heart' that makes a deep impression on others. Model looks are skin-deep, but good-looking hearts radiate from the inside out, putting a smile on your face and kindness in your eyes. A heart that's right with God is the source of true beauty.

Pray

Lord, please change my heart. Please make me more like You, so that when people look at me, they'll see You. Amen.

Sticks and stones ...

'Everyone should be quick to listen, slow to speak and slow to become angry ... Anyone who listens to the word but does not do what it says is like someone who looks at his face in a mirror and, after looking at himself, goes away and immediately forgets what he looks like. But whoever looks intently into the perfect law that gives freedom, and continues in it—not forgetting what they have heard, but doing it—they will be blessed in what they do. Those who consider themselves religious and yet do not keep a tight rein on their tongues deceive themselves' **JAMES 1:19–26**

We all know that **words can and do hurt.** But we often forget in the heat of the moment, when our self-worth is challenged by a nasty remark, to hold back from retaliating with even more malicious words. Arguments can cause so much unnecessary pain and here in our reading today, we see just how we can fix this problem.

James has some advice on dealing with conflict.

- Listen to what the other person is saying. Try to see things from their viewpoint. Often they have a valid point to make which is in your best interest.
- Don't get into a verbal slanging match. Engage your brain before you speak. Don't speak your mind if your mind is not at peace with God.
- Don't lose your cool, either by being aggressive or seething inside. You can't put things clearly when you are cross.

Engage

If you have been upset by remarks others have made about you, ask God to give you the maturity to forgive them. If you are in conflict with anyone else, let God show you the best way to heal the rift. He wants warm hearts, not hot heads.

Pray

Lord, You are the great healer. Please heal any rifts between me and other people. Please help me to forgive other people and say sorry for anything I've done wrong. Amen.

The Confidence Factor

'Jesus Christ laid down his life for us ... we have confidence before God and receive from him anything we ask, because we keep his commands and do what pleases him. And this is his command: to believe in the name of his Son, Jesus Christ, and to love one another as he commanded us. The one who keeps God's commands lives in him, and he in them.' **1 JOHN 3:16–24**

'Confidence' comes from two Latin words meaning 'with faith'. If our belief is in ourselves then failure, rejection or bad experiences can shatter our confidence.

The Christian's confidence is **not self-confidence but confidence in God** and what He can do in us and through us. It's our faith in the goodness of God and His willingness to help us that gives us strength of character. We may not feel up to it, but we know He is!

Have you ever had a crisis of confidence? You gave in to temptation or tried to run away from a problem rather than trust God? Remember: 'I can't – but God can!'

God is able to do incredible things for you and through you. Do you believe that? Put your confidence in God. It's impossible for Him to fail! He is always a winner! Ask Him to make you into a God-confident person. Hold your head up high, look the world straight in the face and go boldly where God wants you to go.

Strong as a rock

'When Jesus ... asked his disciples ... "Who do you say I am?" Simon Peter answered, "You are the Messiah, the Son of the living God." Jesus replied, "Blessed are you ... And I tell you that you are Peter, and on this rock I will build my church and the gates of Hades will not overcome it. I will give you the keys of the kingdom of heaven' **MATTHEW 16:13–19**

Everyone has strengths and weaknesses. Sometimes we can be so aware of our weaknesses that we feel worthless. They say that for every put-down we receive, we require nine compliments to pick us up again. But did you know that **God can turn weaknesses into strengths?**

Jesus was aware of Simon's weaknesses – his tendency to be a bit impulsive, aggressive or cowardly – but He still chose him as leader of the Early Church. He renamed him 'rock', for with the help of the Holy Spirit to turn his weaknesses into strengths, Peter had rock solid leadership qualities. Look at the list opposite and see how our weaknesses are often positive qualities that are being misused.

Simon	**Rock**
THE WEAKNESS	**THE WEAKNESS AS A STRENGTH**
Mischievous, crafty, day-dreaming	Creativity
Conceited, cocky	Confidence
Reckless, brash	Courage
Fanatical, over-bearing, aggressive	Enthusiasm
Impatient	Efficiency
Wishy-washy, spineless, indecisive	Flexibility
Squandering, extravagant	Generosity
Blunt, outspoken	Honesty
Lack of confidence, self-critical	Humility
Indifferent, permissive, disinterested	Patience
Smooth talking, pushy	Persuasiveness
Hard-headed, stubborn	Resoluteness
Touchy, easily offended, emotional	Sensitivity

Engage

Think of some of your weaknesses. Ask God to fill you with His Holy Spirit and redirect those weaknesses into strengths.

Growing up

'When I was a child, I talked like a child, I thought like a child, I reasoned like a child. When I became a man, I put the ways of childhood behind me. For now we see only a reflection as in a mirror; then we shall see face to face. Now I know in part; then I shall know fully, even as I am fully known.' **1 CORINTHIANS 13:11–12**

Our parents spend the first years of our lives worrying how we are going to turn out and our teen years wondering when we are going to turn in. It can be a tricky time when they say things like, 'When you start acting like an adult I'll treat you like one.'

The transition from childhood to adulthood is often a difficult one. Few really understand what's going on and what makes us tick. There are times when we resent older people restricting what we can and can't do, or implying we are too young to handle some situations properly. Conflict with our parents is common as we grow up. So how do you react when your parents or teachers say you are too young or too irresponsible to do something on your own? Sulk, play up, put the stereo on full volume, slam your bedroom door, hibernate under the duvet?

Paul explained that when he became a man he had to put childish ways behind him. He had to **learn the responsibility that comes with freedom.** He was writing to Christians who were fighting and squabbling, showing off, mistreating each other and misusing sex. Christians need to grow up too. God wants us to show greater love and concern for others. From a childish 'Me first' attitude we need to develop a 'God first' approach to all situations.

Engage

Talk with God about any conflicts you have with your parents or teachers. Even if you disagree with their viewpoint or think it is unreasonable, don't just dismiss it. God wants you to show you are mature by doing what they say and earning their trust.

She's a smart cookie!

'Where is the wise person? ... Has not God made foolish the wisdom of the world? ... God was pleased through the foolishness of what was preached to save those who believe ... For the foolishness of God is wiser than human wisdom, and the weakness of God is stronger than human strength.' **1 CORINTHIANS 1:20–25**

A third of your waking hours is taken up with school and study. So how are you doing? Do you drink at the fountain of knowledge or just gargle?

Our experiences at school can leave a lasting impression on our lives. By now you will have classified yourself as a budding Einstein, pretty average or a few pages short of a textbook.

Paul reminded the Christians in Corinth (some who liked to think they were a bit clever) that **knowing Jesus is the best education you can get.** Understanding all the 'ologies and sciences in the world without knowing Jesus isn't smart at all.

That doesn't mean to say that you shouldn't study hard. God wants you to take a keen interest in everything (apart from evil). But we don't need to feel second-rate if others learn more quickly than we do.

Also, you needn't feel inferior if teachers or pupils put you down for believing in God or trusting the Bible to be true. Paul explains that most clever clogs can't get their minds around Jesus or get to grips with what He has done for them. When it comes to understanding the things of God they are as thick as a builder's sandwich. God gives us wisdom – the ability to know what to do with what we know.

Engage

Thank God for showing you the truth about Jesus and explaining His ways. Talk with Him about any problems you face as you study or work.

Don't go with the flow!

'offer your bodies as a living sacrifice, holy and pleasing to God—this is your true and proper worship. Do not conform to the pattern of this world, but be transformed by the renewing of your mind ... Do not think of yourself more highly than you ought ... in Christ we, though many, form one body, and each member belongs to all the others ... Be devoted to one another in love. Honor one another above yourselves.' **ROMANS 12:1–10**

Once the Holy Spirit has opened your eyes so that you can believe in Jesus and know God, things change. Your mind starts to think differently as the Spirit helps you see clearly. Having your mind renewed is one of the greatest miracles in the universe! Enjoy it!

The world that doesn't know Jesus has a certain way of thinking. It's like a pattern that is impossible to get out of without the Holy Spirit changing things. **The world's pattern is that everybody must try to be bigger, better, stronger, richer,** more clever or more powerful than everybody else. If you think that way, you will never be satisfied. Either you'll think too highly of yourself but deep down be terrified of looking weak, or you'll feel worthless and useless if you don't appear the biggest or strongest. That's why if people don't know Jesus, they have to try desperately to be in with the 'in' crowd, to be popular or wear the coolest clothes. That's the pattern of our world and it's a vicious circle. But **God's pattern is different.** He shows us that we don't have to prove ourselves better than others, because we are loved and valued by the most massive, most powerful and most 'cool' person in the universe – Him!

Engage

Are you feeling stressed about your self-image? It's hard work trying to be one up on everyone else all the time, especially if you always seem to be one down! Fashion and popularity are OK things as long as they don't rule our lives. Take a break! Trust in God's love and you will be free to put others first!

OK ... that's it ... I give up!

'As for you, you were dead ... when you followed the ways of this world ... But because of his great love for us, God, who is rich in mercy, made us alive with Christ ... For it is by grace you have been saved, through faith—and this is not from yourselves, it is the gift of God— not by works, so that no one can boast. For we are God's handiwork, created in Christ Jesus to do good works, which God prepared in advance for us to do.'
EPHESIANS 2:1–10

Imagine young children coming in after playing in a wet garden. They are caked from head to toe in mud. What would happen if instead of going to their parents, they tried to clean themselves up? Well, they'd probably smear the mud all over the place and end up in a worse state than before.

clean

That's exactly what we're like in God's eyes if we think that by a lot of effort and hard work we can make ourselves clean from sin and acceptable to God. Just as the child would go to her parents to let them clean her up and put on clean clothes, so we have to go to God and let Him clean us up. It's impossible for us to be good on our own, so we might as well give up! We can only be clean because of what God has done in us. The only reason that infants looks clean and tidy is because of the work their parents have done in cleaning them up. The only reason that we are saved and have anything good about us is because of the work that God has done in us. That is the right self-image to have. Go ahead, give up!

Pray

Lord, thank You that I don't have to try to get rid of my sin by my own hard work. Thank You for making me free from sin. Amen.

What a lovely temple!

'For we are ... God's building. According to the grace of God given to me, like a skilled master builder I laid a foundation, and someone else is building upon it. Let each one take care how he builds upon it. For no one can lay a foundation other than that which is laid, which is Jesus Christ ... Do you not know that you are God's temple and that God's Spirit dwells in you? If anyone destroys God's temple, God will destroy him. For God's temple is holy, and you are that temple.'

1 CORINTHIANS 3:9–17 (ESV)

I *expect* you have been called many things, but have you ever been called a temple before? It's what the Bible calls you. Does that mean you are large with a golden dome? No, it's actually a great compliment that God is paying you.

In the Old Testament, God was present in a small area of the Tabernacle tent known as the Holy of Holies. It was such a holy place that only the high priest could enter it and he could only do so once a year. When the Temple was built, God moved His presence there and filled it with His power and awesome majesty. The priests were so overcome with the glory of God that they had to stop what they were doing and worship Him.

But when Jesus died, God ripped open the curtain in front of the Holy of Holies. God was no longer in the Temple. Where was He? At Pentecost He sent the Holy Spirit to live in those who believed in Jesus as their Saviour.

Can you believe this? Your body is the temple of the Holy Spirit. **God is alive in you.** He is inside waiting for opportunities to radiate His power and glory through you.

It is an incredible honour and an awesome responsibility.

Engage

Just look at the implications of having the Holy Spirit living within you: 'Do you not know that your body is a temple of the Holy Spirit, who is in you, whom you have received from God? You are not your own; you were bought at a price. Therefore honour God with your body' (1 Cor. 6:19–20). What does it mean to honour God with my body? In what ways can I mistreat the body God has given me? Ask God to clean out your 'temple' and fill your life with Himself.

More on the Holy Spirit in 'Fruit Salad'!

He loves *you*

'And now, dear children, continue in him, so that when he appears we may be confident and unashamed before him at his coming ... See what great love the Father has lavished on us, that we should be called children of God! And that is what we are! The reason the world does not know us is that it did not know him. Dear friends, now we are children of God, and what we will be has not yet been made known. But we know that when Christ appears, we shall be like him, for we shall see him as he is. All who have this hope in him purify themselves, just as he is pure.' **1 JOHN 2:28–3:3**

Today we take one last look in the mirror and reflect on what we have learnt about ourselves and about God.

Three out of four girls say they feel under pressure to be perfect. This kind of pressure can make it very difficult to believe that God accepts us as we are. But remember, it's not enough to simply know that you are accepted because of Jesus: **you need to accept yourself,** otherwise you may prevent God from being able to show His power in your life.

There is no need to be weighed down with bitterness, fear, anger or guilt. God has the power to rid us of anything that saps our enjoyment of Him. And there is no excuse to write yourself off as a failure. **You can achieve anything God asks of you,** in His strength.

With God's Spirit you have everything you need to live a fulfilled life. Just let Him take control. Knowing God's love helps you to accept yourself and reject anything in your life that is not worthy of Him.

Engage

You may not feel being a Christian has made that much of a difference, but be patient, God has not finished with you yet. Don't forget to praise God for the progress He's made in your life so far and realise that 'you ain't seen nothing yet'.

'In the days when the judges ruled there was a famine in the land, and a man of Bethlehem in Judah went to sojourn in the country of Moab, he and his wife and his two sons. The name of the man was Elimelech and the name of his wife Naomi, and the names of his two sons were Mahlon and Chilion. They were Ephrathites from Bethlehem in Judah. They went into the country of Moab and remained there. But Elimelech, the husband of Naomi, died, and she was left with her two sons. These took Moabite wives; the name of the one was Orpah and the name of the other Ruth. They lived there about ten years, and both Mahlon and Chilion died, so that the woman was left without her two sons and her husband.' **RUTH 1:1–5 (ESV)**

A Girl Called Ruth

Let's head back to the bad ol' days of the Judges to admire a Bible heroine – Ruth. Esther, who we'll meet later, was an Israelite living in a foreign land. **Ruth was a foreigner** who came to live in Israel.

Naomi, the pleasant wife from Bethlehem, became a bitter and twisted woman. Life seemed so unfair! It all began when she, her husband and her two sons left Bethlehem in search of food. Why had God allowed the famine? None of them wanted to live among the idol-worshipping Moabites, but what choice did they have?

Then Naomi was knocked for six by the death of her husband. Her sons' marriages to local girls raised further questions … **why had they married foreigners who didn't worship God?** Worse was to come … the death of her two sons. It was emotional dynamite that blew her apart.

Poor Naomi was alone in a foreign land with no one to care for her. She suspected her two daughters-in-law, Ruth and Orpah, would remarry and ditch her. Her smile and pleasant manner were buried under an avalanche of anger, bitterness and hurt. She was certain God had it in for her … didn't He care what she was going through?

Engage

Look ahead to verses 20 and 21. Naomi blamed God for the tragic events that exploded into her life. Is God to blame for the suffering that people face? Discuss this with your friends and leaders at church. Had God 'turned His back' on Naomi? Never! (As we shall discover later.) Whenever you go through a tough time, talk with God. Don't blame Him – hear what He has to say to you.

Wherever you will go

'When Naomi heard in Moab that the
LORD had come to the aid of his people
by providing food for them, she and her
daughters-in-law prepared to return
home from there ... Then Naomi said
to her two daughters-in-law, "Go back,
each of you, to your mother's home ..."
But Ruth replied, "Don't urge me to leave
you or to turn back from you. Where you
go I will go, and where you stay I will stay.
Your people will be my people and your
God my God.' **RUTH 1:6–16**

Ruth had married a Jew but then became a widow.
Who would look after her? To make matters worse, she
had to cope with her embittered mother-in-law, Naomi.
Surely it would be best to look after number one, remarry
a hunky Moabite and send Naomi back to Israel?

Good news at last – there's food in Bethlehem. But will
Ruth and Orpah want to go and live in Israel? The tragic
events had brought the three widows close together,
and Ruth and Orpah agreed to go with Naomi even
though it meant leaving their people and the gods they
worshipped. Before they crossed the border, Naomi gave
them time to reconsider their decision.

Orpah was torn apart. She loved Naomi, but she loved
her old way of life more. She wanted to help Naomi,

but she also wanted to remarry a Moabite. She felt more comfortable worshipping lots of gods rather than getting seriously involved in worshipping the one God of the Israelites. Orpah chose the old rather than the new.

Ruth held on to Naomi. She was serious about worshipping God and trusting her future to Him. **Her old Moabite lifestyle and gods were no longer important.** Nothing was going to stop her remaining loyal to God and Naomi. Marriage? A family? She would put God first and leave those decisions up to Him.

Engage

How loyal are you to God and to those for whom He asks you to care? We often face emotional conflicts of loyalties as we go through life. Both Orpah and Ruth loved Naomi. The difference was in their love for God. Ruth put God first, Orpah left God out. When you face difficult decisions, talk with God. Don't be ruthless – be like Ruth and sort out your priorities.

Diamond in the rough

'So Naomi returned from Moab accompanied by Ruth the Moabite, her daughter-in-law, arriving in Bethlehem as the barley harvest was beginning. Now Naomi had a relative on her husband's side, a man of standing from the clan of Elimelek, whose name was Boaz. And Ruth the Moabite said to Naomi, "Let me go to the fields and pick up the leftover grain behind anyone in whose eyes I find favor." ... So she went out, entered a field and began to glean behind the harvesters. As it turned out, she was working in a field belonging to Boaz'

RUTH 1:22–2:3

Israelite law stated that the poor could enter fields at harvest time to pick up grain, grapes and olives that fell to the floor. The Bethlehem down-and-outs were scrambling over the soil for the barley harvest leftovers. **Ruth and Naomi entered Bethlehem as beggars.** Neither had a husband or sons to support them. Poor Ruth – had she made the right decision? Would she live the rest of her life in the gutter? Did the God she now worshipped care about her? Life in Moab was better than this!

Ruth did not complain. She took the initiative by suggesting she joined the Bethlehem down-and-outs scouring the barley fields for dropped grain. Beggars can't be choosers … or can they? Ruth chose to do all she could to help Naomi. It was sweaty, back-breaking work, **but she stuck at it.**

Our attitude towards the problems we face can make such a difference to the way we handle them. Ruth didn't blame God for her poverty, or give up and head back to Moab. Instead she remained positive, worked hard and shared her hard-earned grain with Naomi. Although she couldn't see how God was working in her life, she trusted He would work things out for her good.

Are you facing a tough situation at the moment? Ask God to help you square up and give you the faith to trust in Him.

A not-so-secret admirer

'Just then Boaz arrived from Bethlehem and ... asked the overseer of his harvesters, "Who does that young woman belong to?" The overseer replied, "She is the Moabite who came back from Moab with Naomi ..." Boaz gave orders to his men, "Let her gather among the sheaves and don't reprimand her. Even pull out some stalks for her from the bundles and leave them for her to pick up, and don't rebuke her." So Ruth gleaned in the field until evening ... She carried it back to town, and her mother-in-law saw how much she had gathered.' **RUTH 2:4–18**

Moabites and Jews had been feuding for many generations. How would the Jews treat Ruth?

Rich Boaz heard about Ruth's loyalty to his relative, Naomi, on the Bethlehem gossip line. Instead of sending the foreign girl to the bottom of the pecking order when he saw her in his fields, he put her at the front. Boaz cheered Ruth by praying that God would shelter her and provide for all her needs.

Back then, Boaz didn't use flowers or chocolate to show his admiration, instead he made these things happen:

• His workers deliberately dropped grain for her without her knowing.

- The men were forbidden to make any suggestive or lewd comments to her.
- She could drink from the workers' water supply.
- He invited her to eat with the Jewish workers, a sign of acceptance.
- She was treated to a huge packed lunch.

Kindness can leap over the barriers of prejudice and misunderstanding.

Ruth's unselfish loyalty to Naomi signalled how much she loved God. It earned her acceptance in the local community and a place in the heart of Boaz.

God is your not-so-secret admirer (v12). He loves to show you that He cares by giving you wonderful gifts and by protecting you from harm. So you don't need to face any problems or hard times alone. Let God be your protection and provider.

Pray

God, thank You for helping me and being my shelter. Thank You for always giving me what I need. Amen.

To the rescue!

'Her mother-in-law asked her, "Where did you glean today? Where did you work? Blessed be the man who took notice of you!" Then Ruth told her ... "The name of the man I worked with today is Boaz," she said. "The LORD bless him!" Naomi said to her daughter-in-law. "He has not stopped showing his kindness to the living and the dead." She added, "That man is our close relative; he is one of our guardian-redeemers." ... So Ruth stayed close to the women of Boaz to glean until the barley and wheat harvests were finished. And she lived with her mother-in-law.' **RUTH 2:19–23**

Naomi was so deeply hurt by her plight that she asked to be called Mara, which meant 'bitter'. So why is a sad, bitter woman praising God?

Naomi praised the Lord for the grain, then revved up the praise a gear when she learnt that it was Boaz who had been kind to Ruth. Boaz was a close relative of the family.

Under Jewish law, a widow was cared for by her sons, and if she did not have sons then one of her husband's brothers had to marry her. In Naomi and Ruth's situation where all these relatives were dead, it was the next closest relative who had an obligation to support them.

If the widow was forced to sell her husband's possessions to make ends meet, this relative was supposed to buy them back (redeem them). But Naomi's closest relative made no effort to help her or Ruth.

Boaz was the next relative in line after him. Would Boaz accept the responsibility of being their 'guardian-redeemer' (technical jargon for the relative who paid out to support a widow)?

Naomi began to realise that God hadn't got it in for her. He did care! If she allowed Him, He would untwist the bitterness that was snarled up in her life.

Jesus is our Redeemer (technical jargon for someone who pays a debt we owe). He settled our account with God by dying on the cross. Naomi praised God for sending Boaz as a redeemer. How are you going to thank God for sending Jesus to save you?

Love, love, love ...

'One day Ruth's mother-in-law Naomi said to her, "My daughter, I must find a home for you, where you will be well provided for. Now Boaz ... is a relative of ours. Tonight he will be winnowing barley on the threshing floor. Wash, put on perfume, and get dressed in your best clothes. Then go down to the threshing floor ..." "I will do whatever you say," Ruth answered ... When Boaz had finished eating ... he went over to lie down ... In the middle of the night something startled the man; he turned—and there was a woman lying at his feet! "Who are you?" he asked. "I am your servant Ruth," she said ... he replied "... don't be afraid. I will do for you all you ask ..." When Ruth came to her mother-in-law ... she told her everything ... Then Naomi said, "Wait, my daughter"' **RUTH 3:1–18**

Ruth's 'guardian-redeemer' was supposed to marry her and try for a family so that the family name of her dead husband would pass to the next generation. Why didn't Boaz propose to Ruth? He thought she was wonderful.

Boaz knew that a closer relative was entitled to be her guardian-redeemer before he had a look in. He also doubted that Ruth would want to marry him. Yes, he had money, but he was hardly the pin-up of Bethlehem, and he was getting on a bit. There were plenty of younger hunks around for Ruth to date. He did not want to pressurise Ruth into a relationship that was not based on mutual love.

In the end, Ruth took the initiative and asked him to marry her. Boaz was heart-thumpingly pleased, but didn't draw Ruth into a passionate clinch. Before he ordered his wedding suit (or was it a dress in those days?), **he needed God to give the green light to the relationship.** And that meant making sure he did not upset the relative with the first claim to be Ruth's guardian-redeemer.

Engage

After Ruth and Boaz's first date, Naomi advised Ruth to be patient and not rush ahead of God's plans for her life. When we allow God rather than our passions to control our relationships, we and other people are often spared a lot of hurt and misunderstanding.

Pray

Lord, thank You that You have the best plan for me. Help me to not let my feelings lead me. Instead I choose to follow Your leading. Amen.

Here comes the bride

'Meanwhile Boaz went up to the town gate and sat down there just as the guardian-redeemer ... came along. Boaz said, "Come over here, my friend, and sit down." ... Then he said to the guardian-redeemer, "Naomi, who has come back from Moab, is selling the piece of land that belonged to our relative Elimelek. I thought I should bring the matter to your attention and suggest that you buy it in the presence of these seated here and in the presence of the elders of my people. If you will redeem it, do so. But if you will not, tell me, so I will know ... I am next in line."' **RUTH 4:1–4**

Will Boaz get his bride or will the relative with the better claim to be Ruth's guardian-redeemer whisk her up the aisle?

There were two parts to the contract if you wanted to be Ruth and Naomi's guardian-redeemer.

1. You agreed to buy the land belonging to Naomi's former husband and sons, so it was kept in the family.
2. You agreed to marry Ruth and start a family so the family name of her dead husband could be passed on to the next generation.

The unnamed relative with the first option on the contract liked the deal until he read the small print in section 2. He wanted the land but he did not want a Moabite wife and children who would have a claim on his property.

Boaz moved in to sign the contract (or hand over his sandal, as they did in those days). **He didn't care so much about the land,** he had plenty already, **but he did care about Ruth.** He then did a hotfoot shuffle to tell her the good news!

Engage

Boaz acted as redeemer because he loved Ruth. He didn't enter the deal to get but to give. Jesus is our Redeemer. He paid the price needed so we could enter God's family. Jesus didn't surrender a sandal to settle the deal, He gave His life for us. Thank Jesus for redeeming you. Thank Him for putting your name in God's family records – never to be erased!

cared

A bundle of joy!

'So Boaz took Ruth and she became his wife ... the LORD enabled her to conceive, and she gave birth to a son. The women said to Naomi: "Praise be to the LORD, who this day has not left you without a guardian-redeemer ... For your daughter-in-law, who loves you and who is better to you than seven sons, has given him birth." Then Naomi took the child in her arms and cared for him ... And they named him Obed.' **RUTH 4:13–17**

Ruth had put God first and cared for her embittered mother-in-law at the expense of staying with her own people and raising a family. Now she was to discover that **God always honours those who honour Him.**

Ruth and Boaz were thrilled when God gave them a baby boy. The family line would continue! Naomi just couldn't believe it! She was a grandmother! Her friends were delighted for her.

Naomi could now look back on the traumatic experiences of the past and realise that God had been helping her all along.

She had feared being alone, but Ruth had stayed with her.

She had feared being destitute, but Boaz had provided for her.

She had feared the future, but she now held a little grandson.

The women of Bethlehem who witnessed the sufferings of Ruth and Naomi, praised God for His goodness to them. Naomi had a grandson to cuddle and love. Ruth had a loving husband and family. Boaz had an heir. **God is good!**

When we are sucked into a whirlwind of self-pity, life gets in such a spin that we can easily get things out of focus. We have no idea where we are heading. Instead of holding on to God, we often shut Him out of our lives, even blaming Him for our mistakes and the mistakes of others. Put God first in your life as Ruth did. Hold on to Him. Trust that He really does honour those who honour Him.

The happiest 'ever after'

A GIRL CALLED RUTH

'This, then, is the family line of Perez: Perez was the father of Hezron, Hezron the father of Ram, Ram the father of Amminadab, Amminadab the father of Nahshon, Nahshon the father of Salmon, Salmon the father of Boaz, Boaz the father of Obed, Obed the father of Jesse, and Jesse the father of David.' **RUTH 4:18–22**

Our final episode of Ruth appears to be an anticlimax. It's a list of obscure names in the family tree of Boaz and Ruth. But take a good look. There is an amazing ending to Ruth's story.

Boaz and Ruth were delighted when God gave them a baby boy. But Boaz, the guardian-redeemer, and Ruth, the foreigner who trusted God, had no idea what part they were playing in God's greater plans.

One of their great-grandsons, David, would become king of Israel – the greatest king of Israel! A king who would lead the nation to love, obey and praise God.

But wait … there's more!

Two of David's descendants would be Mary and Joseph. Yes, **Ruth and Boaz were great, great** (and lots more great) **grandparents to Jesus!**

What an honour for Naomi, the woman who thought God had it in for her. What an honour for Ruth, the foreigner – a descendant to save all nationalities. What an honour for Boaz the guardian-redeemer to be in the same family line as the greatest Redeemer!

Engage

What has God been teaching you from the book of Ruth? Take time to thank Him now and ask Him to give you His power to help you put what you've learned into action.

Pray

Lord God, thank You for everything You've taught me through Ruth. Please change me because of it. Amen.

honour

'Praise be to the God and Father of our Lord Jesus Christ, the Father of compassion and the God of all comfort, who comforts us in all our troubles ... For just as we share abundantly in the sufferings of Christ, so also our comfort abounds through Christ ... We do not want you to be uninformed, brothers and sisters, about the troubles ... this happened that we might not rely on ourselves but on God, who raises the dead ... On him we have set our hope that he will continue to deliver us, as you help us by your prayers.' **2 CORINTHIANS 1:3–11**

When people want to check that a microphone is working they often say, 'Testing! Testing!' God sometimes does the same to us. He allows us to experience challenging, often difficult, and maybe distressing things so we can learn how to trust Him when the pressure is on. Here's a survivor's guide to 'Testing! Testing!' times.

God never promises Christians the easy life. Jesus faced tough times and His followers can expect the same.

Paul was honest about the messes in which he found himself and his feelings about them too. He didn't pretend he 'had it all together'. Far from it. He experienced what it was like to be under such pressure that he reached breaking point – despair! He thought his number was up.

It wasn't until Paul realised that he couldn't cope that he asked God to see him through. And in the turmoil he discovered what a loving and comforting Father God is.

In fact, he got really excited about it. He learnt that God is the God of ALL comfort. More than that **He can comfort us in ALL situations.** The logic is simple: if God has the power to raise the dead (v9), then He can help us when we are troubled.

In life's rough times Paul learnt that it was silly to put on a brave 'I can cope' face when he could turn to God for hope, comfort or help. He also learnt that his problems weren't all bad. They taught him to be patient and rely on God. His sufferings made him sensitive to the sufferings of others. He wanted to comfort those who were facing similar problems. So whenever your life comes apart at the seams, don't let the problem drive you away from God but closer to Him instead.

Why me?

'My son, do not make light of the Lord's discipline, and do not lose heart when he rebukes you, because the Lord disciplines the one he loves ... we have all had human fathers who disciplined us and we respected them for it. How much more should we submit to the Father ... God disciplines us for our good, in order that we may share in his holiness. No discipline seems pleasant at the time, but painful. Later on, however, it produces a harvest of righteousness and peace for those who have been trained by it.'

HEBREWS 12:5–11

When problems gatecrash your life and the 'feel good' factor goes into hiding, it's tempting to think that God has it in for you. Does He really care?

Life's difficulties are a bit like buses. There are none for ages and then three arrive at once. One minute everything is OK and the next there is aggravation everywhere you look. All of a sudden everything seems very unfair and God doesn't appear to care.

That's not true. **God cares deeply about our situation and our feelings.** We are His children and He loves us. So whether the mess we are in is of our own making or not, God is around to help us.

And let's face it, many of our hassles are caused by our independence and doing our own thing.

God doesn't spare us from the consequences of our actions. When we head into trouble we often experience troubles. And instead of being full of the Holy Spirit, we quench His power and become sad – maybe very sad. More than anything He wants us to come and sort the matter out with Him. The result isn't only forgiveness – if we learn our lessons we can enjoy a bumper harvest of peace.

Engage

If we are experiencing tough times we mustn't automatically think that God is punishing us for something we have done wrong. Those who are living closest to God often face the greatest trials. But when we know we are in a mess of our own making, we should sort it out with God right away.

peace

Have faith!

'Therefore I tell you, do not worry about your life ... Can any one of you by worrying add a single hour to your life? ... So do not worry, saying, "What shall we eat?" or "What shall we drink?" or "What shall we wear?" For the pagans run after all these things, and your heavenly Father knows that you need them. But seek first his kingdom and his righteousness, and all these things will be given to you as well. Therefore do not worry about tomorrow, for tomorrow will worry about itself. Each day has enough trouble of its own.' **MATTHEW 6:25–34**

Does your faith shrink in troubled waters? Sometimes our worries can get us down. We can spend so much time fretting about the future that we are robbed of our enjoyment of today. So Jesus has a simple message to us today – fear not!

Sometimes we worry about yesterday. Although we have asked God to forgive us, we can have doubts that He has – especially if today is not working out well. Rely on the facts, not your fears. When God says He forgives, He means it. End of matter.

It's also a waste of time, energy and health to fret about the future. Once again, **rely on the facts, not**

your fears. So what are the facts?

- God will provide everything you need (which is not the same as everything you want). If God can supply food for the birds and kit out the flowers in stunning colours He can look after you – and do it in style.
- **God knows the future and what you'll need.** It's daft to worry about things that might not happen when God has answers for the things that will.

Engage

The only thing worry changes is the worrier, and always for the worse. Knowing the facts helps our faith. And it's faith not fear that puts the smile on our face today. Worry is a sign that our faith is shrinking not growing. When you're robbed by fear it's always an inside job. There is no need to get down about the future because God is already there. Live today for God and put Him first in all you do.

Lean on me

'Therefore, since we are surrounded by such a great cloud of witnesses, let us throw off everything that hinders and the sin that so easily entangles. And let us run with perseverance the race marked out for us, fixing our eyes on Jesus, the pioneer and perfecter of faith. For the joy set before him he endured the cross, scorning its shame, and sat down at the right hand of the throne of God. Consider him who endured such opposition from sinners, so that you will not grow weary and lose heart.' **HEBREWS 12:1–3**

When you're feeling down or under pressure, it helps to talk to other people who understand what you are going through. And Paul knows someone who really does understand.

The Hebrew Christians had suffered in many ways for trusting in Jesus. So in Hebrews 11 the writer reminds them of the Old Testament heroes who had taken a clobbering for obeying God – people like Daniel and Jeremiah. But then he moved on to remind them of the greatest inspiration we have in grim times: someone who faced the biggest test of all, who didn't throw in the towel but went on to finish – and win – the fight. Who? The Lord Jesus Christ!

In the Garden of Gethsemane the sweat rolled off Jesus as He struggled with what death would mean: not only barbaric torture but total rejection by God as He became the sacrifice for our sin. He wanted out, but opted in because it was God's plan for His life. He knew that the agony of the moment was nothing compared to being able to make a way for people to enter heaven.

When we are torn apart by our struggles and sadness, **Jesus understands. He's been there,** done it and come out the other end as a winner. So instead of getting hung up looking at the problem, let's focus on the solution – the Lord Jesus Christ.

Engage

Without Jesus to turn to we would soon lose heart and cave in under pressure. That's why it's important to keep talking to Him when the going gets tough. He understands! More than that, He won't let the situation deliver a knock-out punch. With Jesus in your corner you can go the distance and win!

He has the last say

'I consider that our present sufferings are not worth comparing with the glory that will be revealed in us. For the creation waits in eager expectation for the children of God to be revealed ... Not only so, but we ourselves, who have the firstfruits of the Spirit, groan inwardly as we wait eagerly for our adoption to sonship, the redemption of our bodies ... In the same way, the Spirit helps us in our weakness. We do not know what we ought to pray for, but the Spirit himself intercedes for us through wordless groans ... the Spirit intercedes for God's people in accordance with the will of God.' **ROMANS 8:18–27**

War. Starvation. Disease. Crime. Pollution. Each brings its problems. And through no fault of our own we get caught up in the world's suffering. It's a good job God has His own newspaper for us to read.

Independence and disobedience have sprayed graffiti all over God's perfect creation. The planet ticks along but not in the way God intended. The 'God saw that it was good' factor has gone. Sin is a spoiler. And where there's sin there's suffering. Greed means that although there's plenty of food in the world, two thirds of the population suffer from malnutrition – innocent people become victims of war – property is stolen – people die.

Unfortunately, Christians don't have an escape clause from accidents, illness, wars or suffering. Paul describes the whole world as groaning in pain and the situation won't get better until Jesus returns to sort it out. But Christians have a great hope. **No matter how bad things are at the moment it's nothing compared to the great things around the corner** when God takes control. Tears, hurt, failure and pain just won't be able to follow us into heaven.

What's more, there's help for us now when the twists of life take a turn for the worse. When words fail us the Holy Spirit takes up our case with God to comfort and empower us.

Try not to get dragged down by the pain – think of the gain. In all his troubles Paul celebrated the fact that the future was heaven bright! When life seems unfair remember that God will have the last say. If you're so upset about a situation that you don't know what to say, just open up to God and let the Holy Spirit do your pleading.

Strong enough?

'Therefore, in order to keep me from becoming conceited, I was given a thorn in my flesh, a messenger of Satan, to torment me. Three times I pleaded with the Lord to take it away from me. But he said to me, "My grace is sufficient for you, for my power is made perfect in weakness." Therefore I will boast all the more gladly about my weaknesses, so that Christ's power may rest on me. That is why, for Christ's sake, I delight in weaknesses, in insults, in hardships, in persecutions, in difficulties. For when I am weak, then I am strong.'

2 CORINTHIANS 12:7–10

You couldn't ask for a more loyal or dynamic Christian than Paul. So why did God allow Him to suffer some kind of setback, possibly a long-term illness, that he describes as a 'thorn in his flesh'? Surely God would want to keep his key man in peak condition.

A thorn in your skin brings tears to your eyes! You want to get rid of it at once. And Paul felt the same about his condition. But although he had seen God heal others, when he asked God to heal him the eventual answer was 'No'. Why was God being tough on Paul?

Paul began to understand that his success wasn't to do with him but all to do with God. So the fact that he felt weak didn't cut him out of the action. In a remarkable way the weaker he was, the stronger he became – because **he had to rely less on his ability and more on God's.**

And it wasn't as if God had said 'No' and left him to get on with life as best he could. God surrounded His man with all the love, comfort and help he would need to carry on despite the pain.

Any disability is a route into God's ability, providing we are humble. God always gives the humble a head start in life. So if we are unable to function on all cylinders as we like, it's not a barrier to success but a springboard.

Engage

When we face setbacks we often look for someone to blame – and Satan likes to persuade us that it is God's fault when we suffer (some nerve!). God sometimes pulls the 'thorns' out of our lives, and at other times helps us to come to terms with the setbacks we experience. But He's always working to make us better – not bitter. Talk with Him because He really cares.

Don't stop me now!

'And we know that for those who love God all things work together for good, for those who are called according to his purpose ... If God is for us, who can be against us? ... Who shall separate us from the love of Christ? Shall tribulation, or distress, or persecution, or famine, or nakedness, or danger, or sword? ... No, in all these things we are more than conquerors through him who loved us. For I am sure that neither death nor life, nor angels nor rulers, nor things present nor things to come, nor powers, nor height nor depth, nor anything else in all creation, will be able to separate us from the love of God in Christ Jesus our Lord.'

ROMANS 8:28–39 (ESV)

God doesn't say that problems and difficulties are good for us. What's good about setbacks, failure or pain? And if we don't handle them God's way we tend to store up negative thought patterns and attitudes that affect our whole outlook on life. So what does God say? **He says that there isn't a situation He can't use to make us a better person** – more like the Lord Jesus. Our problem or situation may not be good but God can bring good out of the problem. Remember that a diamond is only a lump of coal that was put under pressure for years and years. We face tough times and God teaches us things we could never learn when everything is just great. You can't become a good sailor without facing a storm at sea, or a good athlete without getting some sprains and bruises. Nor can you grow like Jesus without taking some of the knocks Jesus took.

Engage

So what may seem like a kick in the teeth at the time is a great opportunity to tap into God's power and reap the benefits. God works to bring you good, so don't shut Him out. Talk with Him about the things that concern you. Invite Him to get working on the problem but don't be surprised when He starts working on you – for your good!

Pray

Jesus, thank You for being with me when life gets hard. Please help me to stick with You in the tough times. Amen.

Search for a Star

'This is what happened during the time of Xerxes ... For a full 180 days he displayed the vast wealth of his kingdom and the splendour and glory of his majesty. When these days were over, the king gave a banquet, lasting seven days, in the enclosed garden of the king's palace, for all the people ... There were couches of gold and silver on a mosaic pavement of porphyry, marble, mother-of-pearl and other costly stones. Wine was served in goblets of gold, each one different from the other ... By the king's command each guest was allowed to drink without restriction' **ESTHER 1:1–8**

Forget all those talent shows on TV, the story of **Esther is the greatest talent-search story you will ever hear.** It's an epic tale of greed, ambition, hatred and love. How will our heroine get through it?!

Introducing head judge ... the king!

King Xerxes, also known as Ahasuerus, was Mr Big in the powerful empire of the Medes and Persians. He ruled over 127 provinces stretching from Egypt to India that included many Jewish slaves. King Xerxes was the most powerful man in the world and he wanted everyone to know it.

Anybody who was anybody was invited to the 'mother of all feasts', a blow-out meal that lasted for six months. In between courses the guests were entertained by Xerxes showing off his wealth and power. They duly applauded their leader as he let off esteem. After the king's 'I am the greatest' one-man show, there was the party to end all parties. It was stylish, lavish and extravagant. The guests fed their bodies while the king fed his ego.

Engage

The emptiest person is the person who is full of themselves. Do you like to boast about the things you own or can do? God doesn't want you to have a superiority complex (or an inferiority complex). Appreciating God and giving Him the credit for all He does in your life will keep your head small and your heart big. Why not tell Him now how much you appreciate Him?

appreciation

Enter ... the queen!

'On the seventh day, when King Xerxes was in high spirits from wine, he commanded the seven eunuchs who served him ... to bring before him Queen Vashti, wearing her royal crown, in order to display her beauty to the people and nobles, for she was lovely to look at. But when the attendants delivered the king's command, Queen Vashti refused to come. Then the king became furious and burned with anger.' **ESTHER 1:10–12**

The king is completely full of himself and not really thinking straight. He has bragged about his wealth and power. Now he wants to show off his beautiful wife to make the other men envious.

But the long-suffering queen has taken about as much as she can of her self-centred husband and decides to humiliate him by staying put.

The king's ego is deflated like a balloon. He is shown up – a real loser. How dare she do this! Xerxes is steaming with anger and wants revenge.

So he issues a royal decree that banishes Vashti from his presence – forever! He used his power to punish her. His actions satisfied his hurt pride, but did nothing to mend their broken relationship.

When people hurt us, it's so easy to be like Xerxes. Instead of going to talk the matter through with the person, we blab to others to get them on our side. We may not have the power of King Xerxes to punish those who hurt us, but we often let them know we're never going to be friends with them again.

Engage Is there anyone you are not talking to at the moment because you have fallen out with them? Don't get stuck in a moment. Ask Jesus to help you forgive them. Then, if you need to, go and sort out that problem with that person.

elationship

A king without a queen

'Later when King Xerxes' fury had subsided ... the king's personal attendants proposed, "Let a search be made for beautiful young virgins for the king ... Then let the young woman who pleases the king be queen instead of Vashti." This advice appealed to the king, and he followed it ... Before a young woman's turn came to go in to King Xerxes, she had to complete twelve months of beauty treatments prescribed for the women, six months with oil of myrrh and six with perfumes and cosmetics ... She would not return to the king unless he was pleased with her and summoned her by name.' **ESTHER 2:1–4,12–14**

There was now a vacancy for Queen of the Persian Empire. Who would the king choose? He wanted the most beautiful woman in the world.

The king was a male chauvinist where women were concerned, treating them as objects for his pleasure. So he saw nothing wrong in forcing the best-looking girls in the empire to leave their families and spend the rest of their lives in the palace. **They would be well looked after, but only valued for their appearance.**

Do we still think like that today? Hands up if you have drooled over someone just because they are good looking? Or spent hours in front of the mirror wishing your nose was shorter or your legs were longer? Remember that God values people for who they are, not the way they look, and we should do the same.

Here are some topics to discuss with your friends at church:

- **What fashions and looks are in and out at the moment?**
- **Who decides which looks are fashionable and which are out of date?**
- **How can our desires to have the most fashionable look affect our relationship with God and other people?**
- **How should we value other people?**

Why not jot down your thoughts!

Auditions here!

'Now there was ... a Jew ... named Mordecai ... Mordecai had a cousin ... This young woman, who was also known as Esther, had a lovely figure and was beautiful ... Esther also was taken to the king's palace ... Esther won the favour of everyone who saw her ... Now the king was attracted to Esther more than to any of the other women, and she won his favour and approval ... So he set a royal crown on her head and made her queen instead of Vashti.' **ESTHER 2:5–17**

Who's that girl? No one seems to know much about her but she is stunningly beautiful and popular with the judges.

Esther had million-dollar looks, but she was no material girl. Her parents, poor Jewish slaves, had died when she was young and her kind older cousin Mordecai had brought her up. Jews were despised by many Persians and so Esther kept her nationality a secret.

She was probably the only contestant who worshipped God and that gave her a different outlook on life to the others.

The atmosphere at the auditions was undoubtedly competitive and spiteful at times, but Esther didn't provoke any jealousy. When her turn came to parade before the king, all the other girls said how stunning she looked.

Esther not only won the competition, but was also given the star role of Queen of the Empire! Proud, status-conscious King Xerxes had no idea he was marrying the daughter of humble Jewish slaves.

Engage

As Christians we often find we're following a different set of rules to our friends. When we allow Jesus to make a difference to our lives, others soon get to notice. Get together with God now and ask Him to make the difference in your life.

difference

On tour with Esther ... Mordecai

'Esther had not revealed her nationality and family background, because Mordecai had forbidden her to do so. Every day he walked to and fro near the courtyard of the harem to find out how Esther was and what was happening to her.'

ESTHER 2:10–11

When the book of Esther is read to a Jewish congregation, they cheer whenever the name Mordecai is mentioned. Some might say he's our rock 'n' roll star. Let's find out a bit more about our unlikely hero.

When his uncle and aunt died leaving a young orphaned daughter, Mordecai (yea!) came to the rescue. He took on the responsibility of looking after the young girl who had been given the Persian name Esther, meaning 'star'. At that time, Mordecai had no idea what a star she would turn out to be. Esther's real name was 'Hadassah', a Jewish name meaning 'myrtle'. Why was Esther preferred to Hadassah? Well, it could lead to being nicknamed 'Myrtle the Turtle'! The real reason for her Persian name was that **neither Mordecai nor Esther wanted it to be generally known she was Jewish,** as some Persian officials hated the Jews.

Mordecai worked as a guard at the palace gate. Although he was strictly forbidden to go near the *Search for a Star* contestants, every day he went out of his way to find out how Esther was doing. How reassuring it must have been for Esther to know that there was someone nearby who cared for her.

Esther could not see Mordecai but could get messages to him. God is someone we cannot see but we know He is a caring heavenly Father who takes an interest in all we do. Have you got a message about how you're doing to pass on to Him today? Go let it out – tell God how you're feeling. Maybe He has a message for *you*! Spend time with Him now.

Backstage: Mordecai saves the day!
Bigthana and Teresh, like Mordecai, were royal bouncers standing guard to prevent uninvited guests entering the palace. When Mordecai heard them plotting an assassination of the king he reported it to Esther – and the king acted swiftly when he found out. He sent his two disloyal bouncers to the gallows and noted Mordecai's name in his diary.

Cue Haman

'All the royal officials at the king's gate knelt down and paid honour to Haman, for the king had commanded this concerning him. But Mordecai would not kneel down or pay him honour. Then the royal officials at the king's gate ... told Haman about it to see whether Mordecai's behaviour would be tolerated, for he had told them he was a Jew. When Haman saw that Mordecai would not kneel down or pay him honour, he was enraged. Yet having learned who Mordecai's people were, he scorned the idea of killing only Mordecai. Instead Haman looked for a way to destroy all Mordecai's people, the Jews, throughout the whole kingdom of Xerxes.'

ESTHER 3:2–6

Whereas Mordecai gets a cheer each time he is mentioned in a Jewish synagogue, the character we meet today is booed and hissed (the story reaches pantomime proportions)!

Haman (hiss, boo) presented Mordecai (Mexican wave) with a problem. When the ambitious Persian got promoted to No. 2 in the land, he wanted people to worship him. His attitude was, 'Hey man, I'm Haman, get down on your knees'. Mordecai knew he would be expected to put his nose to the dust each time Haman went through the palace gates, but decided that **he would only worship God** – even if it meant he swung from the gallows. When Haman discovered that Mordecai was a Jew, he sizzled with rage. He hated the Jews and stormed off to figure out a way to rid the empire of all those who worshipped God.

Haman craftily persuaded the king that getting rid of the Jews would be the best thing since Persian carpets. He argued that they lived to obey God rather than the king and were a threat to national security.

Do you bow to pressure others put on you to do wrong? It's never easy when you are the only one in the crowd that wants to do it God's way. Talk with God about the pressures on you to drift into no-go areas for Christians. Ask God for His power to stand up for Him today.

Thank God for Christians all over the world who are ready to stay loyal to Him even when it puts their lives in danger. Pray for those who are facing hardship and suffering because they are known to be followers of Jesus.

To shine or not to shine ...

'Esther summoned Hathak ... and ordered him to find out what was troubling Mordecai ... Mordecai told him everything that had happened ... and he told him to instruct her to go into the king's presence to beg for mercy and plead with him for her people. Hathak went back and reported to Esther ... Then she instructed him to say to Mordecai, "All the king's officials and the people of the royal provinces know that for any man or woman who approaches the king in the inner court without being summoned ... [would] be put to death unless the king extends the gold sceptre to them and spares their lives ..." When Esther's words were reported to Mordecai, he sent back this answer: "... who knows but that you have come to your royal position for such a time as this?"'

ESTHER 4:3–14

Mordecai turned yellow when he heard that a decree had been issued to destroy God's people. The orders could not be changed. He was distraught. Was this the end?

Mordecai took the whole terrible mess to God and shed many tears as he begged for help.

It then occurred to him that God might have provided the answer before the trouble arose – Esther. After all, she had the contacts. Surely God had not let her become queen just to live in luxury? Had God put her in this position so she could thwart Haman's plans? Maybe **God was in control** of the situation after all.

He relayed messages to Esther telling her that she must trust God and force a meeting with the king. Esther knew that her life would be at risk if she barged into the king's chambers without being summoned. Remember that no one at the palace knew she was a Jew or what she believed. Perhaps it was best to keep it that way. She faced the hardest decision of her life. **Should she keep quiet or speak out for God?**

Engage

At times it is hard to believe that God is in control of difficult situations. Often it is only as we look back many years later, we see that God had provided an answer before the problem arose. If you are unsure about anything, talk it over with God.

Pray

Father, help me to trust You no matter how tough the circumstances. Help me to speak up for You when You want me to. And thank You for being in control in all situations. Amen.

Show time!

'On the third day Esther put on her royal robes and stood in the inner court of the palace, in front of the king's hall. The king was sitting on his royal throne in the hall, facing the entrance. When he saw Queen Esther standing in the court, he was pleased with her and held out to her the gold sceptre that was in his hand ...

Then the king asked, "What is it, Queen Esther? What is your request? Even up to half the kingdom, it will be given you." "If it pleases the king," replied Esther, "let the king, together with Haman, come today to a banquet I have prepared for him." ... So the king and Haman went to the banquet Esther had prepared. As they were drinking wine, the king again asked Esther, "Now what is your petition? It will be given you ..." Esther replied, "My petition and my request is this ... let the king and Haman come tomorrow to the banquet I will prepare for them. Then I will answer the king's question."' **ESTHER 5:1–8**

After her 72 hours of prayer and fasting, Esther knew she had to play her part and gatecrash the king's throne room without an invite. If he did not hold out his golden sceptre to welcome her, she would face the execution squad. Would she be able to keep her head?

Had those three days of prayer been a waste of time?

No, it was love at first sight. The moment the king saw Esther he couldn't get her out of his head. Instead of demanding her death for entering the inner court without being summoned, he was delighted to see her – he even offered to give her half his kingdom!

Esther could have been diverted by the pound signs lighting up in her eyes … half the kingdom … but **she stayed with the plan God had worked out.** She invited the king and Haman to a dinner party (one she had prepared earlier). Once again she was given the opportunity to ask for whatever she wanted. Designer clothes? Holidays? Expensive jewellery? Esther stuck to God's game plan. The time was not yet right to plead for the Jews. God had other things to do first …

Engage

It's so easy to be diverted away from the course of action God wants you to follow. Esther must have been tempted to think of herself and a more outrageous lifestyle, but she put God first. Is anyone or anything diverting you away from God at the moment? Talk to God about whatever it is and ask Him to keep you on the right track for action that pleases Him.

The results are in ...

'That night the king could not sleep; so he ordered the book of the chronicles, the record of his reign, to be brought in and read to him. It was found recorded there that Mordecai had exposed Bigthana and Teresh ... who had conspired to assassinate King Xerxes. "What honour and recognition has Mordecai received for this?" the king asked. "Nothing has been done for him," his attendants answered ... Now Haman had just entered the outer court of the palace to speak to the king about impaling Mordecai on the pole he had set up for him ... the king asked him, "What should be done for the man the king delights to honour?" Now Haman thought to himself, "Who is there that the king would rather honour than me?" So he answered the king, "... Let them robe the man ... and lead him on the horse through the city streets ..." the king commanded Haman "... do just as you have suggested for Mordecai the Jew, who sits at the king's gate."' **ESTHER 6:1–10**

God is in total control of the situation and the king is reminded how Mordecai saved his life. God knew that the best time for Mordecai to be rewarded for his actions was now – **God's timing is always brilliant!**

Bad man Haman, thinking that the king wanted to reward *him*, suggested a display of public recognition fit for a prince. Imagine his horror, just at the moment he wanted to execute Mordecai, to find he was in charge of honouring him. It was the ultimate show up.

Then imagine Haman's horror when he learnt that Esther was a Jew, worse still that she was related to Mordecai. He had unknowingly sentenced the queen to death – not the best way to further your career at the palace, you can be sure. And in a dramatic turn of events, Haman was led out to swing from the gallows he had prepared for Mordecai. Then Mordecai was led in to be honoured with Haman's job and wealth.

God alone can make the first last and the last first. **He tells the proud to beat it and elevates those who are humble and obedient.**

Engage

Are you putting yourself in a position to be lifted up or brought down? If you are going along with God, listening to His advice and carrying out His plans, you can expect great things. If you are shutting Him out and heading up your life, God may well challenge you and deflate your ego.

Pray

Father God, thank You that I can talk to You all the time. Help me to use that privilege every day. Forgive me for anything I have done wrong and help me to learn what to do each day. Amen.

A fighting performance

'Esther again pleaded with the king ... She begged him to put an end to the evil plan of Haman ... King Xerxes replied to Queen Esther ... "Now write another decree in the king's name on behalf of the Jews as seems best to you, and seal it with the king's signet ring – for no document written in the king's name and sealed with his ring can be revoked." At once the royal secretaries were summoned ... The king's edict granted the Jews in every city the right to assemble and protect themselves ... The day appointed for the Jews to do this ... was the thirteenth day of the twelfth month, the month of Adar. ... the edict was ... made known to the people of every nationality so that the Jews would be ready on that day to avenge themselves on their enemies.' **ESTHER 8:3–13**

Haman may have been out of the way, but the order to annihilate the Jews on the thirteenth day of the twelfth month still stood. The laws of the Medes and Persians could never, never be changed.

Haman's decree could not be altered but Esther and Mordecai persuaded the king to pass another law. **The Jews would have the right to gather together and defend themselves** against any who dared to attack them. (An interesting fact: Esther 8:9, telling how news of the new decree reached the Jews, is the longest verse in the Bible.)

Engage

Christians have the same rights today in our battle with God's enemies. It is important that we meet regularly with other Christians to encourage each other and pray together. Those who are strong Christians can help those who are weak. Christians also need to defend against the temptation to do wrong. That is why it is so important to read the Bible, talk to God and trust Him. Quite often things can start going wrong and it takes us ages before we realise, 'Uh-oh, I haven't really been talking to God recently or reading my Bible – why don't I give it a try?' Prayer and reading our Bible shouldn't be our last resort, they should be our number one priority. If an athlete only trained once a year, how many championships do you think she'd win? We need to keep ourselves spiritually fit.

Pray

Ask God now to help you stay fighting fit by spending time with Him more often.

A reason to sing!

'On the thirteenth day of the twelfth month, the month of Adar, the edict commanded by the king was to be carried out ... The Jews assembled in their cities in all the provinces of King Xerxes to attack those determined to destroy them. No one could stand against them, because the people of all the other nationalities were afraid of them. And ... because fear of Mordecai had seized them ... Mordecai the Jew was second in rank to King Xerxes ... and held in high esteem by his many fellow Jews, because he worked for the good of his people and spoke up for the welfare of all the Jews.' **ESTHER 9:1–3; 10:3**

The thirteenth day of the twelfth month arrived. Would the Jews be annihilated or has God been at work again?

God used the nine months leading up to 'annihilation day' to build Mordecai's reputation. He made a powerful impact at the palace and on the leaders of the provinces. On the dreaded 13th, many Persians sided with the Jews because they respected Mordecai. Others stayed out of the fighting because they were afraid of the Jews. Those who attacked were crushed by God.

It was an incredible victory. Annihilation day had become D-Day – deliverance day!

Engage

It's so easy to forget the great things God has done for us. We too faced a death sentence (cut off from God forever because of our disobedience) until Jesus our Saviour rescued us. The book of Esther is an epic story of God's power, yet God's name is never mentioned. God works behind the scenes to care for His people. What have you learnt from Esther? What has God been quietly doing behind the scenes in your life?

Pray

Take time out today to show God your appreciation – thank Him for saving you.

Fruit Salad

'But the fruit of the Spirit is love, joy, peace, forbearance, kindness, goodness, faithfulness, gentleness and self-control. Against such things there is no law. Those who belong to Christ Jesus have crucified the flesh with its passions and desires. Since we live by the Spirit, let us keep in step with the Spirit. Let us not become conceited, provoking and envying each other.' **GALATIANS 5:22–26**

The first Christians lived in a hot Mediterranean climate ideal for growing fruit. So when Paul was explaining how the Holy Spirit changes people he told them about the special fruit God had planted in their lives.

You can't grow a melon in a day. Oranges don't ripen overnight. And the Holy Spirit doesn't turn frogs into princes in an instant.

God definitely wants you to **become more like the Lord Jesus.** How? By allowing the Holy Spirit to have more influence over your thoughts and actions. There's just no way round it. **And it takes time.**

Over the next few days we're going to munch through these characteristics of Jesus. Many of them are linked: love involves kindness; peace brings joy. This is not an accident. The Holy Spirit produces fruit, not fruits. These qualities are not separate things, but one – the character of Jesus.

Engage **The Holy Spirit lives within Christians to help them grow more like Jesus. Ask God to fill you with the Holy Spirit so others notice the difference. Remember that God wants fruit not religious nuts!**

qualities

Sweet love

'Dear friends, let us love one another, for love comes from God. Everyone who loves has been born of God and knows God. Whoever does not love does not know God, because God is love. This is how God showed his love among us: he sent his one and only Son into the world that we might live through him. This is love: not that we loved God, but that he loved us and sent his Son as an atoning sacrifice for our sins. Dear friends, since God so loved us, we also ought to love one another. No one has ever seen God; but if we love one another, God lives in us and his love is made complete in us.' **1 JOHN 4:7–12**

First on the list of the fruit of the Holy Spirit is love. But what is love? We use the word in so many ways ... to describe the way we feel about our parents, the opposite sex, our favourite crisps, our best pizza topping, our pet hamster ... So what kind of love are we on about here?

Parts of the Bible were originally written in Greek, and the Greeks used three different words for love. The kind of love that said, 'Phwoah, check out that bit of alright', was called **'eros'**. It is a selfish desire to get, not to give. The kind of love that said, 'That's an OK person', was called **'phileo'**. It is a close friendship between people who get on well together. The third kind of love – the one listed as a fruit of the Holy Spirit – is called **'agape'** (pronounced ag-ap-ay). **It is love that gives without looking for anything in return.**

Eros says, 'Gimme what I want.' **Phileo** says, 'I'll like you if you like me.' **Agape** says, 'I love you no matter what.' God's love is **agape** love. Despite the way we ignore Him, He still cares deeply about us. It was **agape** love that took Jesus to the cross to die so we could enjoy God's forgiveness. And it's **agape** love the Holy Spirit brings to our lives. It helps us to love the unlovely and help the helpless.

Jesus was betrayed, deserted and disowned by His friends. He was framed by corrupt officials. He was slapped, punched, whipped, ridiculed and spat at. Then He was led out to be cruelly crucified, having done nothing wrong. And how does He react? Is He bitter? Is He out for revenge? No, He shows the ultimate in **agape** love by asking God to forgive them. Yes – forgive them!

Engage

Corinth was a gross city full of *eros* attitudes. Paul reminded the Christians there that Holy Spirit love was kind, patient, truthful and loyal (1 Cor. 13). Jesus shows us that love is also forgiving. Ask God to fill you with agape – 100% pure love – the love that has the power to forgive.

Joy overload!

'Holy Father, protect them by the power of your name, the name you gave me, so that they may be one as we are one. While I was with them, I protected them and kept them safe by that name you gave me ... I am coming to you now, but I say these things while I am still in the world, so that they may have the full measure of my joy within them ... Sanctify them by the truth; your word is truth. As you sent me into the world, I have sent them into the world.' **JOHN 17:11–18**

The Holy Spirit brings joy to Christians. What is joy? Is it that feeling of elation that makes us jump, laugh and scream when we've got great results back from an exam? Joy is more deep-rooted than that. It's not so much about what you do but who you know.

A full measure of corn was a sack filled to the top, shaken to let the contents settle and refilled to overflowing. A full measure of joy is when the Holy Spirit packs so much happiness, peace and contentment into your life that it spills out. But Holy Spirit joy is much more than that 'yes factor' when things are going your way. He doesn't take you into overdrive one minute and reverse the next as situations change. **Such deep happiness isn't dependent on**

your circumstances but on your relationship with God.

Jesus spoke about joy hours before He was crucified. How could He do that? He understood that the secret of joy is obeying God. Jesus was prepared to face the pain and rejection of crucifixion because of the 'great joy' that would result. He also knew His disciples would face hurt and suffering too, so He prayed that they would have a 'full measure of joy' – filled, shaken and overflowing – as they obeyed God.

Engage

The excitement of knowing God deepens as we obey Him. Joy comes from doing what God wants us to do; saying what God wants us to say; being where God wants us to be; going where God wants us to go. Talk with God and find out more about His plans for your life. JOY is Jesus first, Others next and then Yourself.

A slice of peace

'Jesus replied, "Anyone who loves me will obey my teaching. My Father will love them, and we will come to them and make our home with them ... All this I have spoken while still with you. But the Advocate, the Holy Spirit, whom the Father will send in my name, will teach you all things and will remind you of everything I have said to you. Peace I leave with you; my peace I give you. I do not give to you as the world gives. Do not let your hearts be troubled and do not be afraid."' **JOHN 14:23–27**

Turmoil! Stress! Strain! Hassle! Aggro! Fighting! War! Tune in to the news and you'll see that peace is in short supply. Yet among all the unrest Christians can enjoy a peace that defies explanation. How? See what the Prince of Peace says.

You lie back in your sunlounger, sip a cool drink and mutter, 'Ahh, peace at last!' But in reality that's a cue for a wasp to start divebombing you, a neighbour to rev up his lawnmower, a cloud to cover the sun and the sunlounger to collapse. Such peace is easily shattered! **Peace in the world is very fragile, fickle and unpredictable.** All kinds of things can leap out and unsettle us. Teachers for one! You arrive at school in a good mood and suddenly they hassle you for your homework. Why do they do that? Families are another. You are watching the TV in peace when someone switches the channel ... need I say more?

The peace that the Holy Spirit brings to our lives is not dependent on people around us but the Person inside us. It's **the peace of Jesus,** who faced the most stressful situations with a deep inner calm. It's a peace that **comes from obeying God and knowing you are safe in His care!**

Engage

Have you heard of the phrase, 'no peace for the wicked'? Well it's true! (See Isa. 48:22.) Those who go against God's ways won't ever know His peace. It's not until we have peace with God that we can know the peace of God.

peace

How to make a Patience-Fruit Punch

'The LORD had said to Abram ... "I will make you into a great nation ..." God also said to Abraham, "As for ... your wife ... I will bless her and will surely give you a son by her. I will bless her so that she will be the mother of nations; kings of peoples will come from her." Abraham fell face down; he laughed and said to himself, "Will a son be born to a man a hundred years old? Will Sarah bear a child at the age of ninety?" ... Now ... the LORD did for Sarah what he had promised. Sarah became pregnant and bore a son to Abraham in his old age, at the very time God had promised him.'

GENESIS 12:1–2; 17:15–17; 21:1–2

One thing a fruit grower needs is patience. You'd need to be a few pips short of a pomegranate to rush out just after planting and pluck the blossoms. Yet we can be a bit like that with the fruit of the Holy Spirit. We want God's benefits but we want them now – if not yesterday!

Have you ever got impatient with God? Maybe He hasn't answered your prayer yet? Abraham learnt that you sometimes need to wait patiently for God to act.

God began by renaming Abraham 'the father of many'

at a time when he didn't have children. Imagine being known as 'Big Daddy' when you are 75 years old and it appears that you and your wife can't have children. Many years passed, and when it became obvious that Sarah would not have millions of descendants their patience ran out. Abraham, with Sarah's permission, had an affair with a servant girl to get the son he wanted. He was called Ishmael. But this hasty action (as you might have guessed) brought trouble and tension to the family.

It was not until Abraham was 100 years old that God miraculously gave him and Sarah a son – Isaac. If only Abraham had waited patiently for God he could have saved himself and the world a lot of trouble. Ishmael's descendants became known as Arabs, Isaac's descendants became known as Jews. And Abraham's descendants are still fighting among themselves today.

Engage

Some of the biggest mistakes in life are made when we rush headlong into decisions, without waiting for God to show us the right moves to make. We become more like Jesus by waiting patiently for God to do things in God's way and in God's time.

Ripe with kindness

'When the Son of Man comes in his glory ... he will separate the people one from another as a shepherd separates the sheep from the goats. He will put the sheep on his right and the goats on his left. Then the King will say to those on his right, "Come, you who are blessed by my Father; take your inheritance, the kingdom prepared for you since the creation of the world. For I was hungry and you gave me something to eat, I was thirsty and you gave me something to drink, I was a stranger and you invited me in ..." Then the righteous will answer him, "Lord, when did we see you hungry ... or thirsty ...?" The King will reply, "Truly I tell you, whatever you did for one of the least of these brothers and sisters of mine, you did for me."' **MATTHEW 25:31–40**

Kindness is like snow; it makes everything it covers white and clean. It is a language that the deaf can hear and the blind can see. It's the oil that takes the friction out of life and the ability to love people more than they deserve.

Greeks were sometimes confused because the word for kindness, 'chestos', sounded like the word for Christ, 'Christos'. They weren't sure whether Christians were followers of Christ or followers of kindness. The answer is both! Christ is kindness.

In Acts 9:36 we hear of a great example of kindness. Dorcas, a Christian lady who may have been a widow herself, put her faith into action by getting out her sewing needle. She spent hours making clothes for orphans and those in need. **Her kindness was the talk of the town.** As she sewed her cloth she also sowed the good news of Jesus. People wanted to know why she cared. No one else did. They were drawn to her, then drawn to Jesus.

Engage

Do you realise you can be kind to God? When we are kind to a person in need, we are being kind to ... guess who? Yes, to God Himself. Who are the modern day equivalents of the people Matthew mentions? That unpopular person in your class? That scruffy, smelly person no one wants to sit next to? Mmm ... being kind to God is harder than it sounds. Kind actions begin with kind thoughts. The Hebrew word for kindness means 'to bow the head and treat courteously'.

Pray

Father, help me to value people as You do. Help me to think well of them and show, through kindness, my thoughts becoming my actions. Amen.

Full of goodness

'Give thanks to the LORD, for he is good ... to him who alone does great wonders ... who by his understanding made the heavens ... who spread out the earth upon the waters ... who made the great lights ... the sun to govern the day ... the moon and stars to govern the night ... He remembered us in our low estate ... and freed us from our enemies ... He gives food to every creature ... Give thanks to the God of heaven. *His love endures forever.'* **PSALM 136:1–26**

Today we look at another quality of the Holy Spirit and learn how to become someone who 'clings on' to good (Rom. 12:9).

No one wants to be thought of as some kind of teacher's pet. So what does it mean to be good? The word means many things. If a girl shoots her grandmother with a peashoooter from a distance of 100 metres we would call her a good shot, but not necessarily a good person. So we need to understand what the Bible means when it talks about goodness.

It doesn't mean doing your best ... helping old ladies across the street ... earning brownie points at school ... as good as these things might be. To understand goodness we shouldn't think about what we do, but about who God is. God is good. Good is God. The two are inseparable.

Goodness is God reaching out.

To bring good to a situation we need to bring God to the situation. Acting and reacting as He would want. Goodness is God-likeness. It's not about our image but His. So don't get hung up wondering what others will think if you do the right thing. Work out what God would want you to do and go for it.

Engage

Being good is not about 'sugar and spice and all things nice'. It is the greatest challenge of the Christian life. Can you bring God into every situation you face today? If you want to be good, start with God.

Pray

Holy Spirit, please fill me. Help me to bring something of God's goodness into every situation. Amen.

goodness

Grow your own

'Elkanah ... had two wives ... Peninnah had children, but Hannah had none ... Because the LORD had closed Hannah's womb, her rival kept provoking her in order to irritate her. This went on year after year ... In her deep anguish Hannah prayed to the LORD, weeping bitterly. And she made a vow, saying, "LORD Almighty, if you will only look on your servant's misery and remember me, and not forget your servant but give her a son, then I will give him to the LORD for all the days of his life ..." ... they brought the boy to Eli, and she said to him, "Pardon me, my lord. As surely as you live, I am the woman who stood here beside you praying to the LORD. I prayed for this child, and the LORD has granted me what I asked of him. So now I give him to the LORD."' **1 SAMUEL 1:1–11,21–28**

Faithfulness is not a word you hear often. Sometimes we hear people talk about being faithful to their marriage partner. That means no sneaking off to have secret affairs. Or you may hear of someone who has given faithful service to a company – a reliable, trustworthy and loyal worker. **God wants us to be faithful – so what does that involve?**

Hannah couldn't have children and in the days when a woman's worth was judged by the size of her family, that was bad news! She made a solemn promise that if she had a son, she would give him back to God to train as a helper at the tabernacle. When God answered her prayer and Samuel was born, one would hardly have blamed her if she had had second thoughts and kept her son at home. She must have been emotionally blown apart when she handed young Samuel over to become Eli's assistant. Poor Mum would only see her boy once a year.

It's no light thing to make a promise – to God or anyone else. Hannah was faithful and kept her promise, and God was also faithful to Hannah. He gave her other children. And as for Samuel, he became very important in God's plans. It was a time when the leaders of Israel were doing their own thing. So rather than speak to the priests, God spoke to young Samuel. The boy became God's voice to the nation.

So how reliable are you? Homework springs to mind. Do you faithfully do it and hand it in on time? When you say you will keep your bedroom tidy does it then look as if a herd of wildebeests has stampeded through it? God wants us to be faithful in the way we handle the everyday matters. And when we have proved we can deliver the goods on small matters, He'll trust us with bigger issues.

Get your dose of Vitamin Humility!

'In your relationships with one another, have the same mindset as Christ Jesus: who, being in very nature God, did not consider equality with God something to be used to his own advantage; rather, he made himself nothing by taking the very nature of a servant, being made in human likeness. And being found in appearance as a man, he humbled himself by becoming obedient to death – even death on a cross!' **PHILIPPIANS 2:5–8**

Some people suffer from 'I' strain. They blow their own trumpet, beat their chest, wave their awards, polish their egos and recount their exploits (with a good deal of exaggeration). A big shot is often a person of small calibre and an immense bore. God isn't like that. He is big enough and strong enough to be humble.

What is humility? Well it's not acting all coy and saying how useless you are. You don't hear Jesus making excuses or running Himself down. Yet He was humble.

Jesus is God, but He never acted as if He was more important than anyone else. He treated people as if they were more important than Him.

He never pulled rank, making out He was right because He knows everything. He listened to people, asked questions and took time to explain. Neither did He brag about His lifestyle in heaven – or look down His nose at the poor and needy. Instead **He gave up the luxurious living of heaven to be born in a stable,** live in a one-bedroom flat in Nazareth, mix with a bunch of no-hopers **and die a cruel death on a cross.** Why? Because He put us before Himself. He gave up all His rights and privileges to obey God. Meekness is not weakness. You have got to be tough to be humble.

Engage

There's nothing wrong with being good at things, and knowing it, as long as it doesn't make us think we are better or more important than others. Spend time today thanking God for all the things you are good at. Also remember that it is God who has given you your abilities and they are to be used to bring praise to Him, not yourself. Stay humble or you will stumble.

humble

Seeds of self-control

'Then Jesus went with his disciples to a place called Gethsemane, and he said to them, "Sit here while I go over there and pray." ... Going a little farther, he fell with his face to the ground and prayed, "My Father, if it is possible, may this cup be taken from me. Yet not as I will, but as you will." Then he returned to his disciples and found them sleeping. "Couldn't you men keep watch with me for one hour?" he asked Peter. "Watch and pray so that you will not fall into temptation. The spirit is willing, but the flesh is weak."

MATTHEW 26:36–41

Self-control is the ability to eat just one crisp (one of those that comes in a cardboard tube and rhymes with jingle!). Impossible, eh? It's hard to say 'no' when your body is shouting 'yes' and hard to say 'yes' when your body is screaming 'no'. Just look at the battles for control over self that took place in the Garden of Gethsemane.

Peter, James and John had had a good meal, a few glasses of wine and it was getting late. When Jesus asked them to stay awake and pray, they did their best but nodded off to sleep. It wasn't that they didn't want to pray – they did, but when they closed their eyes they drifted off. Their spirits were willing but their bodies were weak.

Just look at the colossal struggle that Jesus had. His body was weak. And His spirit was weak. The suffering He was about to go through on the cross played on His mind. His spirit was deeply troubled at the thought of being cut off from God as He became a sacrifice for sin. **Every part of His human body was shouting, 'No, give up. Don't go through with it.'** But Jesus took the struggle to God and said, 'It's not what I want but what You want that counts.'

Engage

We rarely set out to lose control and give in to temptation. It just happens and we're too weak to resist. That's why we've got to talk with God and be honest with Him about our feelings. It's important we make a clear decision to do things His way and ask for His power to say 'no' when our body is shouting 'yes'. Or for the ability to say 'yes' to God when everything else is bellowing 'no'. As we finish making our 'fruit salad' out of the fruit of the Spirit, think about what areas you would like to grow in. And don't forget this 'fruit' is only achieved through being filled with the Holy Spirit – all you have to do is invite Him in!

Get Up and Glow!

'Then the eleven disciples went to Galilee, to the mountain where Jesus had told them to go. When they saw him, they worshipped him; but some doubted. Then Jesus came to them and said, "All authority in heaven and on earth has been given to me. Therefore go and make disciples of all nations, baptising them in the name of the Father and of the Son and of the Holy Spirit, and teaching them to obey everything I have commanded you. And surely I am with you always, to the very end of the age."' **MATTHEW 28:16–20**

Life with Jesus is the only life worth living – but for some reason **it's the best kept secret!** It's our job to change that. Let's see how we can get up and glow for God!

Jesus didn't expect His disciples to stay put but to go. Go where? Everywhere! There was no time to laze in the sun, soaking up the rays, or stay cosy in a nice holy huddle – there was a world out there needing to be told that Jesus was alive!

I wonder how the disciples felt when they realised that gospel begins with GO! Nervous? Tense? 'After you'? 'I don't know what to say'? 'Stop the Church, I want to get off'?

Jesus didn't expect a bunch of brawny fishermen, an 'I'm going straight now' tax collector, a former terrorist and a few hangers on to suddenly turn into smooth-talking evangelists. But with the help of the Holy Spirit they learnt to go and glow, telling those close to them about Jesus, and **soon the world was buzzing with the news.**

Before Jesus told His disciples to 'Go' He reminded them that He was in charge (v18). Jesus has the power to change lives – that's why we go and show Him to others. Jesus then reminded His disciples He would still be with them – ALWAYS – no exceptions, no exclusion clauses in the small print. In the words of a famous song – 'You'll never walk alone!' Even when dying on the cross, Jesus wanted the thief dying next to Him to know who He was. He practised what He preached. Ask Him to help you get up and glow for Him. When we go for Jesus, others come to Jesus.

Pray

Lord Jesus, make me ready to go for You, whatever that means for my life. Amen.

That's the Spirit!

'When the Advocate comes, whom I will send to you from the Father – the Spirit of truth who goes out from the Father – he will testify about me. And you also must testify, for you have been with me from the beginning.' **JOHN 15:26-27**

Glowing for Jesus is not so much a question of what you know but who you know. You don't need to know the Bible back to front and have a smile that looks as if you slept with a coathanger in your mouth to introduce others to Jesus. **But you do need the Holy Spirit.**

The Holy Spirit is Jesus' greatest fan. He can't wait to cheer, shout, sing, show and tell the world about God's Son. There is no way we could ever match the enthusiasm of the Holy Spirit to go and get 'em for Jesus. Come rain or shine He is rooting for Jesus, which is why we need His help.

The Holy Spirit takes our mumbling, cringing, 'I feel so shown up' words and turns them into hard-hitting statements that affect people more than they will ever let on. He uses our puny attempts to help others to reach the heartstrings other emotions can't reach.

Someone has described glowing for Jesus as 'not our responsibility but our response to His ability'. You see, effective witness is not based on our cleverness, but on our willingness to go with the flow of the Holy Spirit.

Engage

Why not get together with some of your friends and make a list of people you know who don't know Jesus. Then you could all pray for them and ask God to give you opportunities to tell them about Him and show them how much He loves them. This would also be a good time to pray that God would fill you with His Holy Spirit so you can be bold, be strong and know He is with you. THE HOLY SPIRIT IS JESUS' GREATEST FAN.

What's love got to do with it?

'I pray also for those who will believe in me ... that all of them may be one, Father, just as you are in me and I am in you. May they also be in us so that the world may believe that you have sent me ... and have loved them even as you have loved me ... Righteous Father, though the world does not know you, I ... will continue to make you known in order that the love you have for me may be in them and that I myself may be in them.' **JOHN 17:20–26**

Jesus spent three years with His disciples telling them all about God and helping them to follow Him. Why? Just listen in to Jesus' prayer as He prepared to die on the cross.

Jesus introduced His disciples to God so that they would glow for Him and show God's love to others. What is so special about God's love? Human love is often selfish. We can become more concerned with what we get out of love rather than what we can give. We throw love like a boomerang, hoping to get it back. **But God loves us even though He gets nothing in return.**

When the disciples were snubbed by some Samaritans they wanted to stick the boot into them. Jesus reacted differently by loving the Samaritans despite the fact they wanted nothing to do with Him.

Everyone hated tax collectors, they were traitors and cheats. But Jesus surprised His disciples by eating with them. Why? Jesus loves anyone and everyone, without prejudice or selfish interest.

The good news is that we can learn to accept others in the same way. Jesus asked God to give us His love. And it's the Holy Spirit who makes it real to us.

Engage

Jesus went out of His way to meet up with some of the lowest of the low and show them God's love.

Who is the most unlikeable person in your street? In your class? In your church youth group? Pray for them. Ask God to help you love them in the same way that He does.

Spend a little time

'Jesus, tired as he was from the journey, sat down by the well ... When a Samaritan woman came to draw water, Jesus said to her, "Will you give me a drink?" ... The Samaritan woman said to him, "You are a Jew and I am a Samaritan woman. How can you ask me for a drink?" ... Jesus answered her, "If you knew the gift of God and who it is that asks you for a drink, you would have asked him and he would have given you living water." ... The woman said, "I know that Messiah" (called Christ) "is coming. When he comes, he will explain everything to us." Then Jesus declared, "I, the one speaking to you – I am he." ... Many of the Samaritans from that town believed in him because of the woman's testimony' **JOHN 4:5–26,39**

The Samaritans had on a previous occasion refused to welcome Jesus' disciples. Most Jews took a detour round Samaria to avoid any contact with its inhabitants. But not Jesus. **He went out of His way to meet them.**

Just look how Jesus introduced this woman to God. He took the initiative of speaking to her. This came as a bit of a shock ... a Jew speaking to a Samaritan! More shocking ... a Samaritan woman!! Shock, horror ... a Samaritan woman with a bad reputation!!!

As they met at a well, water was the topic of conversation. It was a friendly conversation. Jesus did not preach to her. He asked questions. He listened. He made her think.

Jesus then started to tell her about God by talking about 'living water'. He didn't bore her with His opinions but kept to the facts, gently pointing out that she needed God's forgiveness. Jesus also sidestepped a question about which church He recommended. He was not interested in introducing her to religion but to God! The most important thing to God is not where we worship but who we worship.

Engage

As the woman spent time with Jesus she began to realise who He was and she was so excited she ran off to tell her friends and family the good news.
You may feel that you're not up to telling your friends or family about Jesus.
If so, don't worry. Jesus can help you get alongside people and get to know them. Ask Him to help you get into conversations with people and when the opportunity is right, gossip the gospel.

All the right questions

'Now there is in Jerusalem ... a pool ...
Here a great number of disabled people
used to lie – the blind, the lame, the
paralysed. One who was there had been
an invalid for thirty-eight years. When
Jesus saw him lying there and learned
that he had been in this condition for a
long time, he asked him, "Do you want
to get well?" "Sir," the invalid replied,
"I have no one to help me into the pool ..."
Then Jesus said to him, "Get up! Pick up
your mat and walk." At once the man was
cured; he picked up his mat and walked.'

JOHN 5:2–9

When you have been paralysed for 38 years,
unable to move, begging for a living and feeling totally
helpless, what do you say to a stranger who asks, 'Do you
want to get well?'

Surely Jesus could see the man wanted nothing more
in the world than to get well. **So why did He
ask the question?**

Questions make us think. They force us to kick start
our brains into action. They challenge our second-hand
beliefs. They bring us into the conversation. They invite
us to express our opinions.

Sometimes we think that talking to others about Jesus

means giving all the right answers. It is often better to ask the right questions.

The lame man needed help to get around and he needed help to be made right with God. He told Jesus that he wanted to be healed and Jesus did this. Later, Jesus was able to speak to him about the 'sickness' in his heart.

Here are some questions you could ask to get people thinking:

Who is Jesus?

What is a Christian?

What happens to you when you die?

Can you think of other questions worth trying out?

....

....

....

....

....

....

 Christians sometimes have a surplus of simple answers and a shortage of simple questions. Ask God to prompt you with the right questions for the right people at the right time.

It's all in the preparation

'"But you will receive power when the Holy Spirit comes on you; and you will be my witnesses ... to the ends of the earth." After he said this, he was taken up before their very eyes ... Then the apostles returned to Jerusalem ... When they arrived, they went upstairs to the room where they were staying ... They all joined together constantly in prayer, along with the women and Mary the mother of Jesus, and with his brothers.'

ACTS 1:8–14

When Jesus returned to heaven his last words were about glowing for Him. He promised to send the Holy Spirit to transform His yellow-bellied shirkers into dynamic workers ready to conquer the world. So how did they react when Jesus was out of sight?

After all the trauma of Jesus' death and resurrection it was tempting for the disciples to clear out of Jerusalem and unroll their beach towels by the Sea of Galilee. But Jesus had clearly said that they were to begin witnessing in Jerusalem. What a place to start! It was full of Jesus-haters.

So what did the disciples do? They stopped their knees knocking by getting down on them. They prayed not once or twice, but regularly. Did they ask God to change

His mind? 'Lord – anywhere but Jerusalem!' No, they asked God to send His Holy Spirit.

I wonder if they prayed for Herod? Or Pontius Pilate? Or those who plotted to kill Jesus? Did they pray for the many people who had met Jesus? Listened to Jesus? Been healed by Jesus?

What we do know is that when the Holy Spirit came their prayers were answered and 3,000 people became Christians. **Prayer prepares people for Jesus!**

Talk with God about some of the people you know who need Jesus as their Saviour. List their names on this page (or in the back of your Bible) and pray for them regularly.

....

....

....

....

....

....

....

Talk the walk

'Always be prepared to give an answer to everyone who asks you to give the reason for the hope that you have. But do this with gentleness and respect, keeping a clear conscience, so that those who speak maliciously against your good behaviour in Christ may be ashamed of their slander. For it is better, if it is God's will, to suffer for doing good than for doing evil. For Christ also suffered once for sins, the righteous for the unrighteous, to bring you to God. He was put to death in the body but made alive in the Spirit.' **1 PETER 3:13–18**

Actions speak louder than words. When we are kind, thoughtful and help others it leaves more than a good impression. It leaves question marks as well. And if they ask you why you are so eager to do good ...

Be prepared! **Be ready to make the most of any opportunity when others question you about your beliefs.**

Sadly we are often gobsmacked when asked about being a Christian. We feel awkward and try to avoid the subject. 'Er, yes, that fish badge on my Dad's car ... local angling club, maybe?' Or sound apologetic, 'Well, I sort of go to church ...' Or fudge the issue, 'Well, if you don't change your ways ... a little bit, and repent ... as it were, you will go to hell ... to a certain extent.' Or sometimes we can ram home our views and spark off an argument.

Engage

Peter says that every Christian should know what to say about Jesus and how to say it. Over the next few days we'll look at the things we could say. But before we open our mouths, how did Peter advise us to speak?

Gently – Don't slam-dunk the Bible, or your opinions, on other people's ear drums. Instead, patiently explain what Jesus has done for you.

Show respect – Even though you may disagree with other people's opinions, listen and try to understand their viewpoint.

Peter's advice is very clear. Don't be scared ... put God first ... be good ... do good ... and when you are given an opportunity to chat about Jesus – chat about Jesus. Chat about Jesus as you would chat about anything else that means a lot to you.

Pray

Thank You, God, that there's nothing I can't do with Your help. Please give me the courage to speak up for You. Amen.

Hidden hurt

'As Jesus and his disciples, together with a large crowd, were leaving the city, a blind man, Bartimaeus ... was sitting by the roadside begging. When he heard that it was Jesus of Nazareth, he began to shout, "Jesus, Son of David, have mercy on me!" Many rebuked him and told him to be quiet, but he shouted all the more ... Jesus stopped and said, "Call him." So they called to the blind man, "Cheer up! On your feet! He's calling you." Throwing his cloak aside, he jumped to his feet and came to Jesus. "What do you want me to do for you?" Jesus asked him. The blind man said, "Rabbi, I want to see." "Go," said Jesus, "your faith has healed you." Immediately he received his sight and followed Jesus along the road.' **MARK 10:46–52**

So what do you say to someone who asks you about Jesus? Well, there's no special set of words or magic formula. God promises to help us know the right thing to say at the time. But over the next four days we'll lock onto some key targets.

Bartimaeus was handed a third-class ticket through life when he was born blind. He couldn't see, he couldn't join in activities with other people, he couldn't earn a living. He was trapped in a black hole of rejection. No one seemed to understand or care.

When he shouted to Jesus he was met with a barrage of, 'Shut it! Jesus is too busy for the likes of you' and other unhelpful comments. But these people were wrong – very wrong!

And that's something people today need to know. **Jesus really cares about them.** He loves them just as they are. And He always has time for them.

Engage

You see, some people, deep down, feel God doesn't care about them. Perhaps they have been rejected or hurt by other people – even Christians. Others feel so guilty about the way they have lived they steer clear of anything to do with God, fearing He will tear into them. So don't keep people in the dark, let them know – God loves them, no matter who they are, or what they have done. It is helpful when talking to people to show them a verse in the Bible that explains what you are saying. Learn John 3:16. Underline it in your Bible so you can point out that 'God so loved the world' that He sent Jesus! Repeat the verse aloud to God and ask Him to remind you of the words when you need them.

One way!

'Meanwhile, Saul was still breathing out murderous threats against the Lord's disciples ... As he neared Damascus on his journey, suddenly a light from heaven flashed around him. He fell to the ground and heard a voice say to him, "Saul ... I am Jesus, whom you are persecuting ... Now get up and go into the city ...." Saul got up from the ground, but when he opened his eyes he could see nothing ... In Damascus there was a disciple named Ananias ... Placing his hands on Saul, he said, "... Jesus ... has sent me so that you may see again and be filled with the Holy Spirit." Immediately, something like scales fell from Saul's eyes, and he could see again. He got up and was baptised' **ACTS 9:1–18**

When people realise they're at odds with God they need your help to wise up about His forgiveness. It is sometimes a bit of a struggle to help people realise that Jesus is the one and only – their way to God. Take Saul for example ...

Saul was so sure he could impress God by doing all the right things that he was convinced he didn't need Jesus. He went to church kitted out in his smartly pressed Pharisee outfit, droned long prayers, recited Bible verses and tossed coins into the collection box.

If there was one person Saul thought he could do

without it was Jesus! And most people are the same today. They think that by going to church or confessing to a priest, everything will be hunky-dory. Some think there are many routes to heaven and it doesn't matter whether you are a Buddhist, Hindu, Muslim or Micky Mouse fan, you'll make it through the pearly gates somehow.

It came as a big shock to Saul to realise that Jesus was God's Son. Ananias kindly explained that there was one way to God and Jesus had died on the cross to open up that way. That day, Saul believed in Jesus. **He stopped relying on religion and entered into a relationship with God.** As Saul was later to write, 'There is one person who joins God and man – the Lord Jesus Christ' (based on 1 Tim. 2:5).

Here is another key verse to underline in your Bible, memorise and use. Acts 4:12: 'Salvation is found in no-one else, for there is no other name under heaven given to men by which we must be saved.' There's only one way to God. All other routes are diversions. Ask God to help you know it, believe it and tell it.

When you believe

'About midnight Paul and Silas were praying and singing hymns to God, and the other prisoners were listening to them. Suddenly there was such a violent earthquake that the foundations of the prison were shaken. At once all the prison doors flew open, and everyone's chains came loose. The jailer ... called for lights, rushed in and fell trembling before Paul and Silas. He then brought them out and asked, "Sirs, what must I do to be saved?" They replied, "Believe in the Lord Jesus, and you will be saved – you and your household." ... At that hour of the night ... he and all his household were baptised.' **ACTS 16:25–33**

The word 'believe' is mentioned 99 times in John's Gospel alone! It's one thing to discover that Jesus is the only way to God but it is another thing to believe it. Those searching for God may need our help to understand the decision they need to make. **To believe Jesus or reject Jesus – that is the mother of all questions.**

A Bible translator working with a tribe found that they did not have a word for 'believe'. The closest meaning was the phrase 'throwing your whole weight'. John 3:16 was therefore written as 'whoever throws his whole weight on Jesus will not perish but have everlasting life'.

Paul told the jailer exactly what he needed to do – believe in the Lord Jesus. He then explained what that involved. The prison-hardened jailer learnt that he had to break with his old life and ask God to forgive him. He needed to throw his whole weight on Jesus, trusting Him for everything in the future.

This iron-hearted man melted and told his family he was now for Jesus not against Him. Those who believe in Jesus should tell someone as soon as possible. It's not something to be ashamed of but something to celebrate!

Engage

Hot news! Read 1 Corinthians 1:21. God says He is pleased to forgive those who believe in Jesus. And the whole of heaven joins in the celebrations whenever someone believes in Jesus. If you ever get an opportunity to help someone who wants to know more about Jesus, ask the Holy Spirit to help you and give you the right things to say. Faith is a gift from God and it is that faith which helps someone to believe.

Pray

Holy Spirit, please fill me. Give me opportunities to speak about Jesus, courage to take them, and good words to say. Amen.

Worth it!

'When the LORD restored the fortunes of
Zion, we were like those who dreamed.
Our mouths were filled with laughter,
our tongues with songs of joy. Then it
was said among the nations, "The LORD
has done great things for them." ... Those
who sow with tears will reap with songs
of joy. Those who go out weeping,
carrying seed to sow, will return with
songs of joy, carrying sheaves with them.'

PSALM 126:1–6

Are you keen to tell people that God loves them? ...
that there is the problem of sin to deal with? ... that Jesus
is the only way to God? ... and they need to believe in
Jesus to know God? Possibly not ... but remember, Jesus
promises to send His Holy Spirit to help us glow for Him
– we don't have to rely on our own abilities ... PHEW!

When God calls us to witness to others, He doesn't
promise that it will always be easy. Sometimes it can be
quite hard, and cause us a lot of pain. You see, when we
stand up for Jesus, some people won't like it at all. And
that can sometimes mean being labelled as a whacko or
an oddball. The thought of our mates making fun of us
is not very nice and we'd rather keep quiet in order to
keep our friends. Instead of being life transformers we

slink off to become life accepters – we feel it's easier to leave things as they are.

Don't focus on the pain, look at the gain. Introducing people to Jesus brings great joy. Even when those to whom we witness give us a hard time, God brings deep contentment to our lives. And, surprise, surprise, some people we introduce to Jesus do believe in Him, just maybe not immediately and some much later in their lives. That is definitely something worth celebrating, not only here but in heaven. Remember this – **nothing we do for Jesus is ever a waste of time.** Any pain is short-lived but the gain is forever!

CHECKLIST!!

- **Are you praying for your non-Christian friends?** Keep praying!
- **Are you making an effort to get to know people?** Get alongside them!
- **Are you going out of your way to be kind and helpful to others?** Don't stop!
- **Are you asking God to give you opportunities to chat about Him?** Remember you are not inviting trouble but joy!
- **Do you really believe God will give you the right words to say at the right time?** Well, there's only one way to find out!

Passionate, complete, unfaltering faith ... It's about giving God your all!

God's wise words can change the course of our whole lives if we *wholeheartedly* believe and follow them. This book is bursting with inspiring stories, Bible passages and guiding prayers to help you explore topics such as dealing with pressure and rising up to challenges.

978-1-78259-353-9

See how what you believe about God really does affect your life.

Containing short chunks to chew over and real-life stories which take you through themes including 'The character and personality of God' and 'Getting the best out of life' – real living for (and with) God.

978-1-78259-182-5

YP's daily devotional – dig deeper into God's Word

Never did reading the Bible look so good! Get eye-opening, jaw-dropping Bible readings and notes every day, plus special features and articles in every issue (covers two months).

Available as individual issues or annual subscription. For current prices and to order visit

www.cwr.org.uk/youth

Also available online or from Christian bookshops

Being a Christian sounds great, but what exactly does it involve?

If this is what you have been thinking then this booklet is for you. In just 30 days you can find out how completely mindblowing life with God can be. Each day we explain how you can effectively live for Jesus and start to get to grips with the Bible – His Word to us.

978-1-85345-105-8

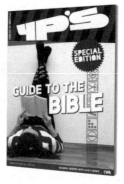

Get to know and understand the Bible

Written to help you know and understand the Bible better, this exciting full-colour guide includes key events, maps, timelines, major characters, explanations of biblical terms and so much more!

978-1-85345-352-6